HANDWRITING FOR MINECRAFTERS

Printing

Illustrated by Amanda Brack

Sky Pony Press
New York

This book is not authorized or sponsored by Microsoft Corp., Mojang AB, Notch Development AB or Scholastic Inc., or any other person or entity owning or controlling rights in the Minecraft name, trademark, or copyrights.

Sky Pony Press books may be purchased in bulk at special discounts for sales promotion, corporate gifts, fund-raising, or educational purposes. Special editions can also be created to specifications. For details, contact the Special Sales Department, Sky Pony Press, 307 West 36th Street, 11th Floor, New York, NY 10018 or info@skyhorsepublishing.com.

Minecraft® is a registered trademark of Notch Development AB.
The Minecraft game is copyright © Mojang AB.

Visit our website at www.skyponypress.com.

10 9 8 7 6 5

Library of Congress Cataloging-in-Publication Data is available on file.

Cover art by Bill Greenhead

Cover design by Brian Peterson

Interior art by Amanda Brack

Book design by Kevin Baier

Print ISBN: 978-1-5107-3253-7

Printed in China

A NOTE TO PARENTS

Parents know just as well as teachers that adding fun to schoolwork helps to motivate kids and enhance their learning.

Handwriting for Minecrafters: Printing is the ultimate in kid-friendly handwriting practice. With their favorite game characters to guide them through the alphabet, kids will be eager to master print letter formation. All it takes is one page of guided practice a day to reinforce what kids are learning in the classroom and encourage continued academic success.

Added features like numbered strokes and traceable practice rows keep frustration to a minimum, build confidence, and help kids learn at a comfortable pace.

Kids who master the alphabet can move on to more advanced practice including writing their name, copying Minecraft-themed words and sentences, and more!

Whether it's the joy of seeing their favorite game characters on every page or the thrill of seeing the progress they're making, this workbook is designed to entice even the most reluctant student.

Happy adventuring!

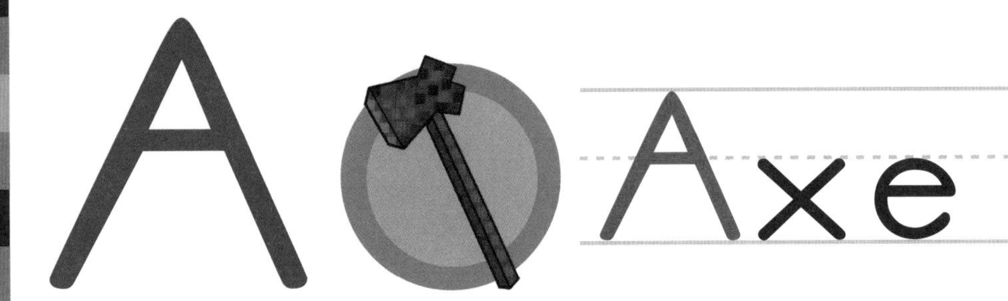

1 2 3
A A A A A

axe

1 a 2

a a a a

B

Bed

1 2 3

B B B B B

b

bed

1 2

b b b b b

C Creeper

c creeper

D

Dog

d
dog
1
2
d d d d

E

Enderman

2
1
3
4

E E E E E

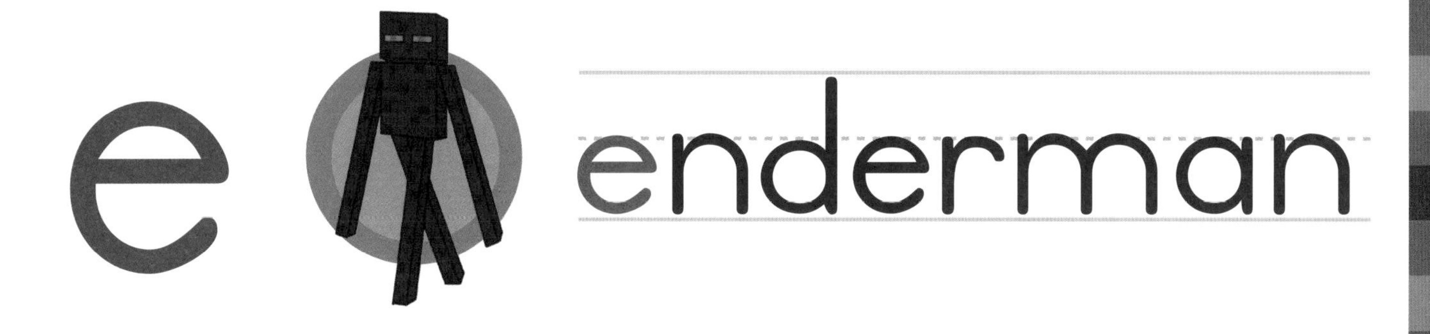

e 1 e e e e

F

Fish

f
fish
1
2
f f f f f

G Ghast

1 g 2

g g g g

H

Helmet

1 3 2

H H H H H

h

helmet

1 2 h h h h h

I

Ice

i

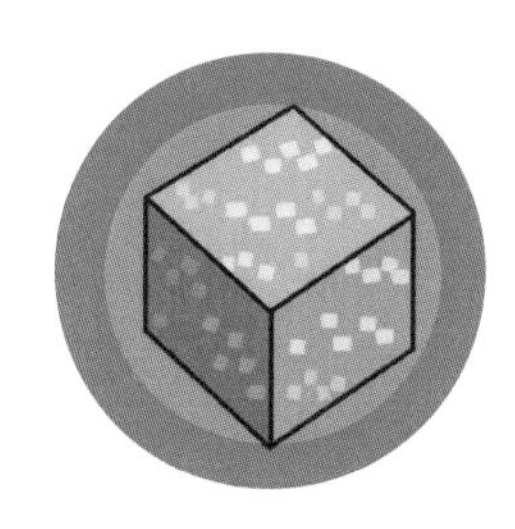

ice

2
1
i i i i i

J
Jack o'Lantern

2
1

j

jack o'lantern

1 2 3

K K K K K

kitten

1 k 2 3

k k k k

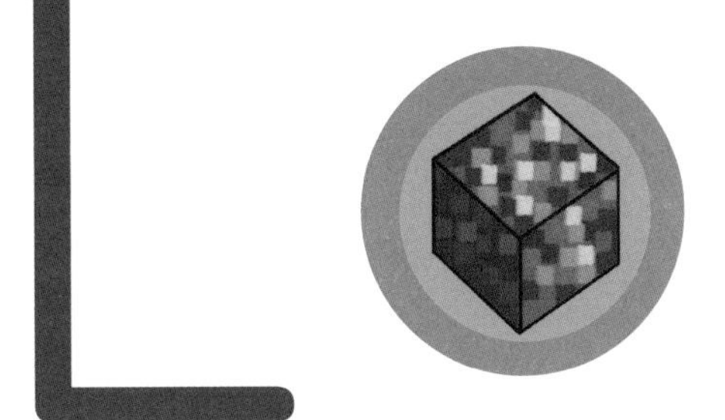

Lava

1 2

L L L L L

l

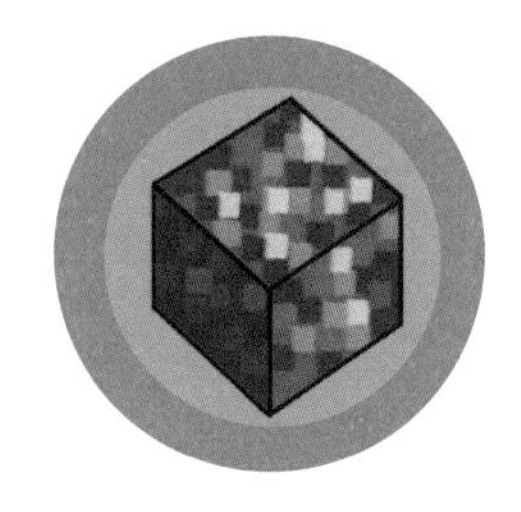

lava

1

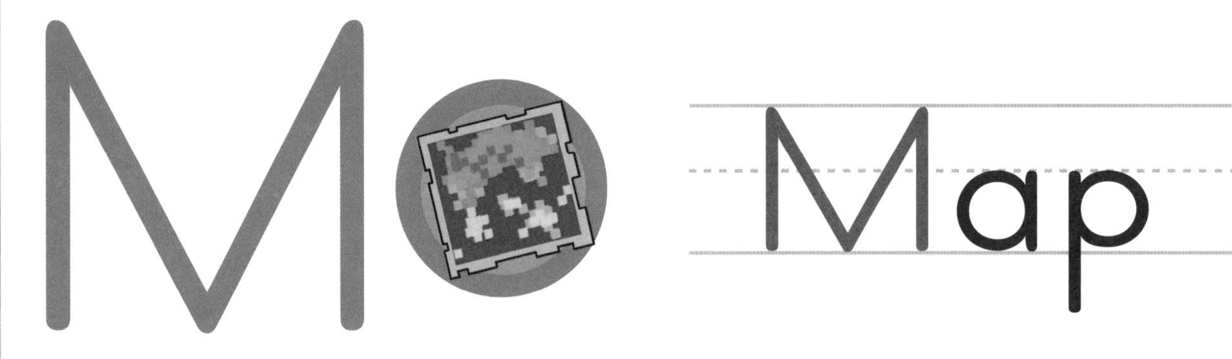

1 2 3 4

M M M M M

map

1 2 3

m m m m m

N
Night

1
2
3
N
N N N N

n night

1 2

n n n n n

Orb
1

O
orb
1

P

Potion

p potion

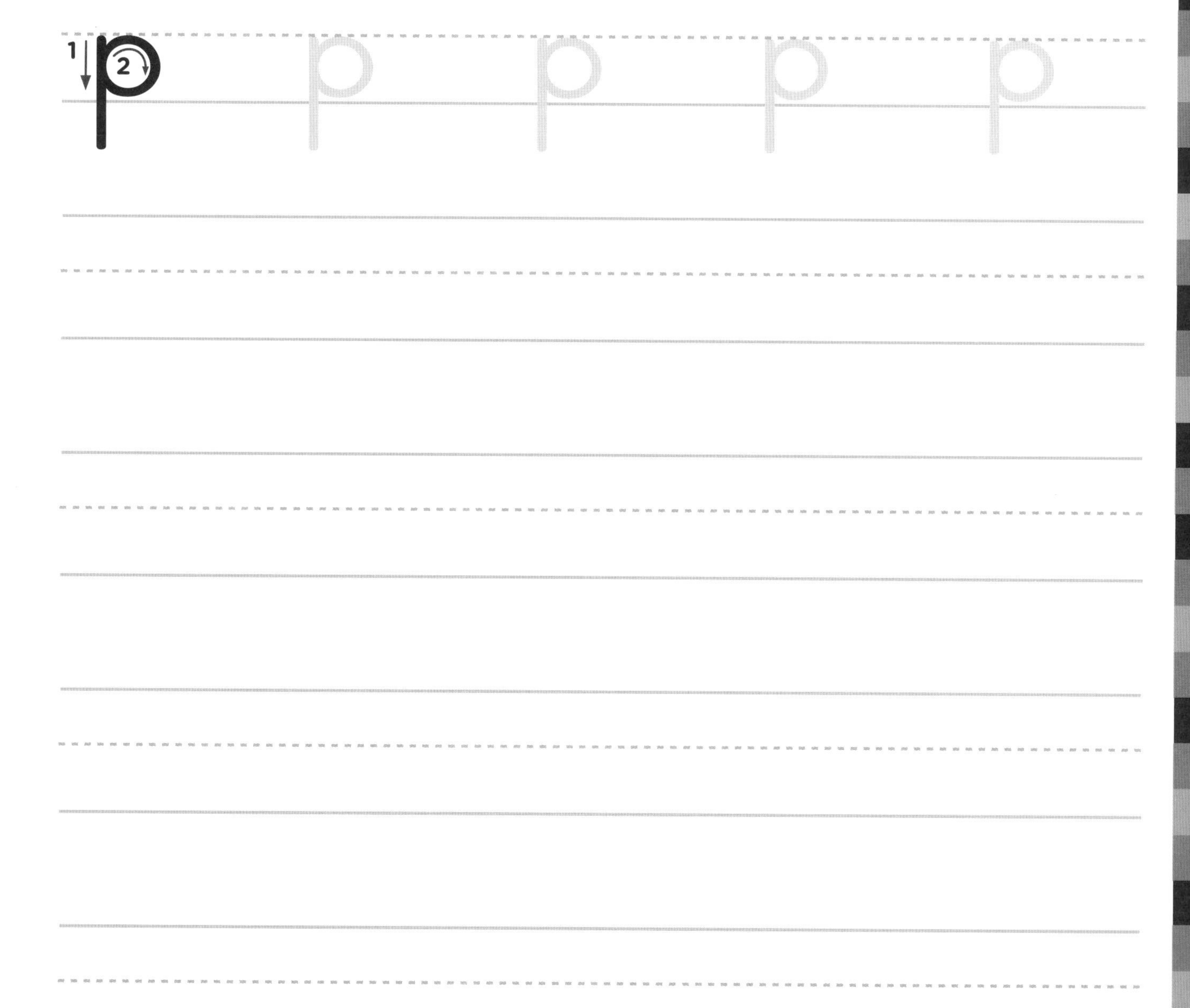

Q 1 2 Q Q Q Q

q 1 2 q q q q

R R R R R

r  railway

1 r 2

r r r r

S

Skeleton

S S S S S

S  skeleton

s s s s s

T

Torch

2

1

T

T T T T

t

torch

1 t 2

t t t t

U
Unpack

1
U U U U U

unpack

1 2
V V V V V

v
villager

1
2
v
v
v
v
v

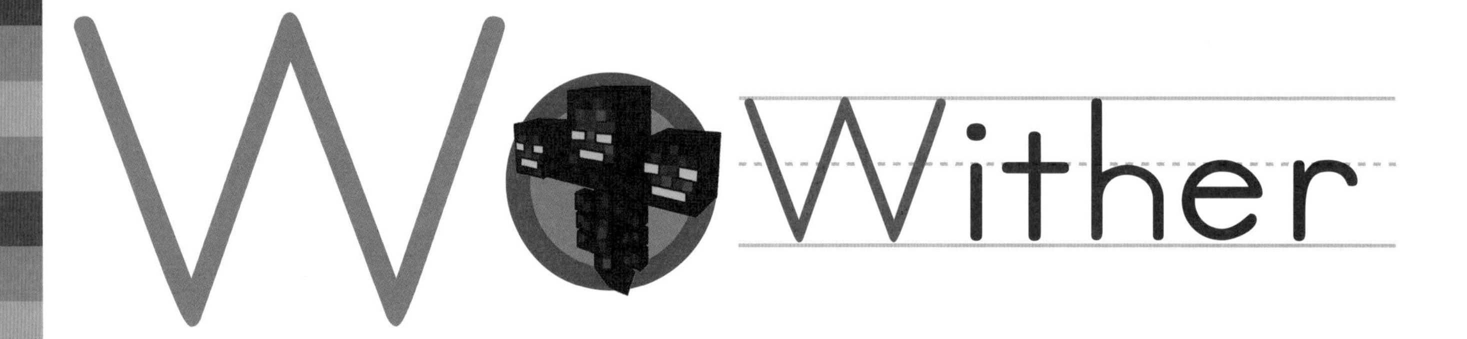
W
Wither

1 2 3 4
W W W W W

1 2 3 4

w w w w w

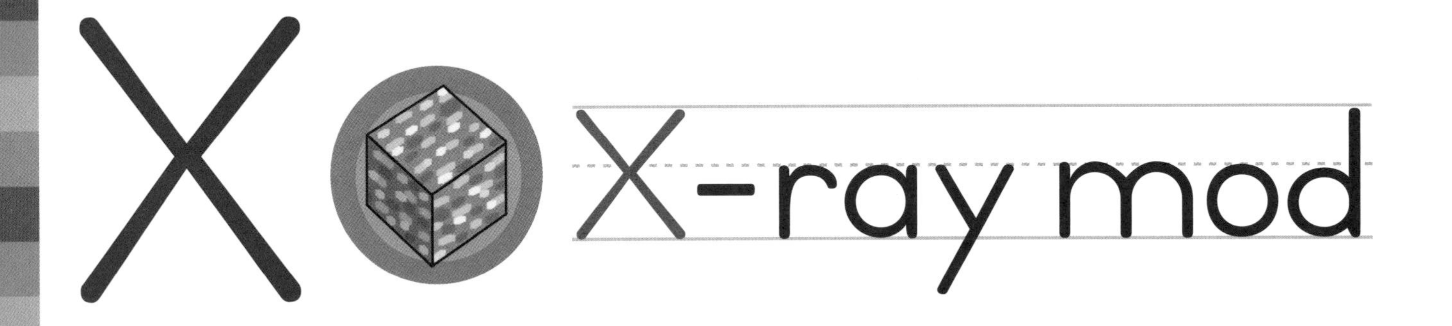

1 2

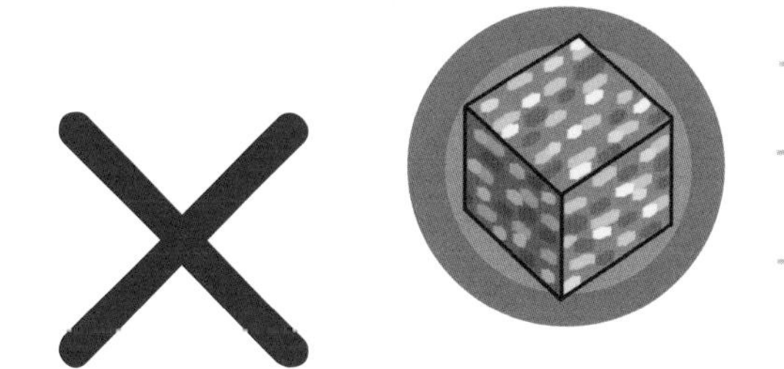

x-ray mod

1 2

x x x x

1 Y 2 Y Y Y Y

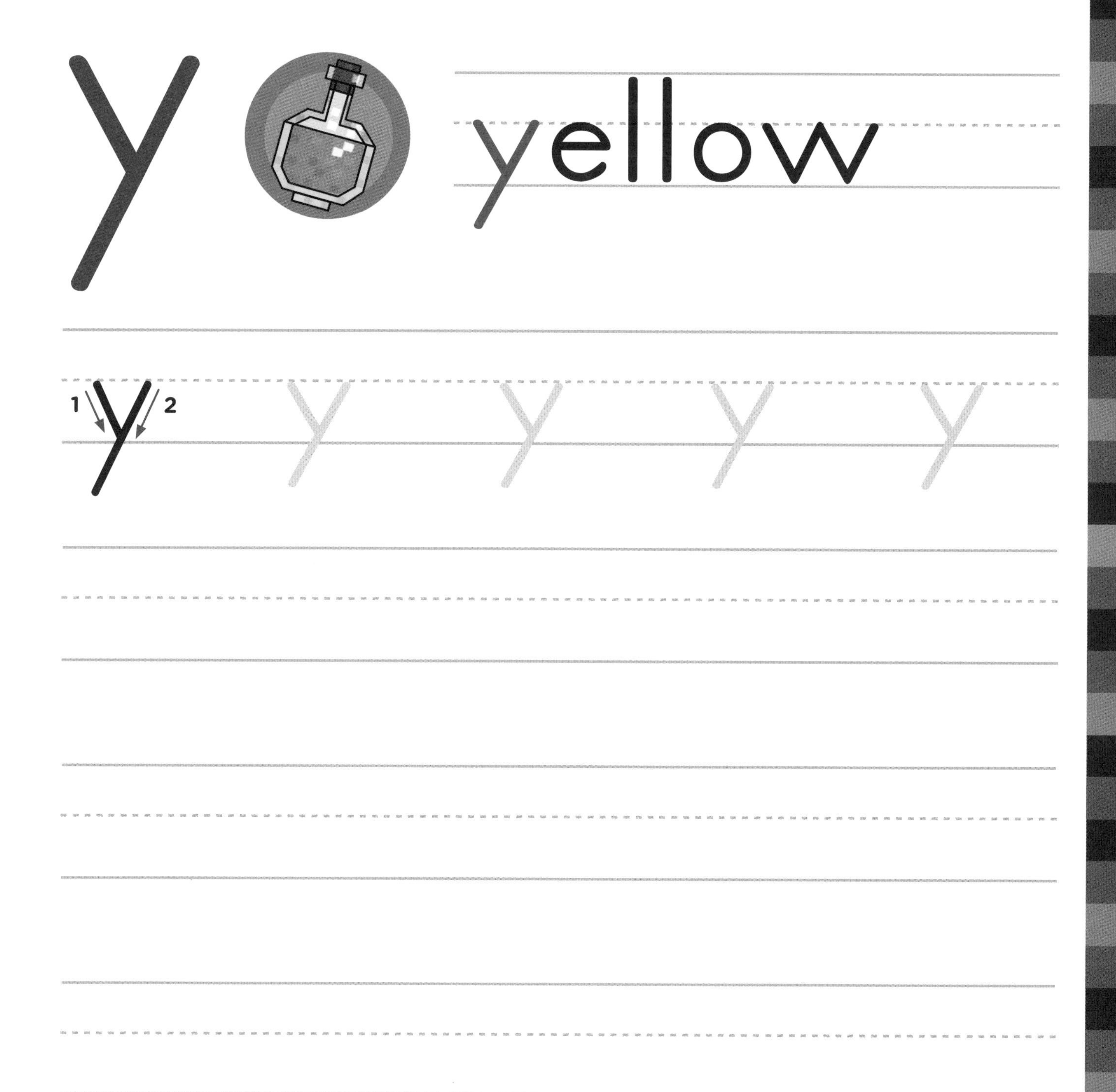
y
yellow
1 y 2

Z

Zombie

1 2 3

Z Z Z Z Z

Z zombie

1 2 3

THE ALPHABET

Trace all of the alphabet letters to review what you learned.

A B C D E

F G H I J

K L M N O

P Q R S T

U V W X Y Z

a b c d e

f g h i j

k l m n o

p q r s t

u v w x y z

NAME PRACTICE

Practice writing your name on the lines below.

WORD PRACTICE

Now practice writing the names of these hostile mobs.

creeper

zombie

wither

skeleton

slime

WORD PRACTICE

Practice writing the names of these passive and neutral mobs.

ocelot

squid

wolf

spider

villager

Steve mined diamonds and crafted these items.
Practice writing the item names.

sword

pickaxe

shovel

Practice writing the name of Alex's enchanted weapon.

bow and arrow

SENTENCE PRACTICE

Copy the Minecrafting sentences below.

Iron golems protect villagers.

Zombies drop rotten flesh.

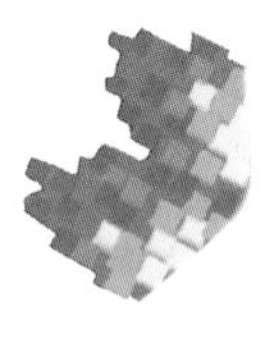

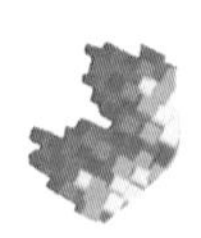

Ghasts shoot fireballs.

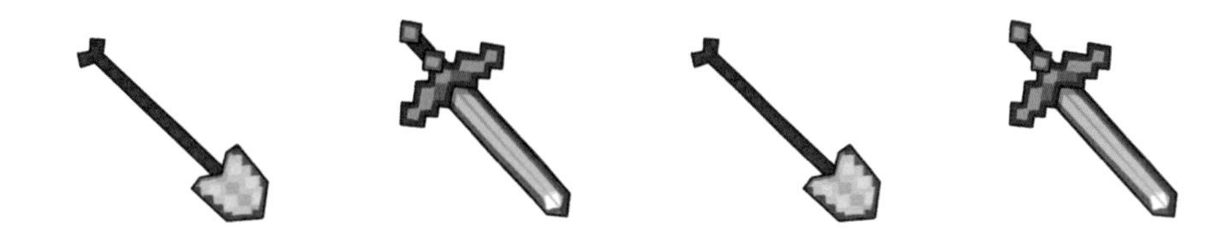

Diamond weapons are strong.

Endermen can teleport.

Creepers hate cats.

Withers are deadly.

Write what you know about Minecrafting in your best print handwriting below! Describe your Minecrafting adventures or write a story about YOUR FAVORITE MOB.